THOUGHT BAG LL

"PER ASPRA, AD ASTRA"

MALIK AAQIB

Copyright © Malik Aaqib
All Rights Reserved.

This book has been published with all efforts taken to make the material error-free after the consent of the author. However, the author and the publisher do not assume and hereby disclaim any liability to any party for any loss, damage, or disruption caused by errors or omissions, whether such errors or omissions result from negligence, accident, or any other cause.

While every effort has been made to avoid any mistake or omission, this publication is being sold on the condition and understanding that neither the author nor the publishers or printers would be liable in any manner to any person by reason of any mistake or omission in this publication or for any action taken or omitted to be taken or advice rendered or accepted on the basis of this work. For any defect in printing or binding the publishers will be liable only to replace the defective copy by another copy of this work then available.

To My Loving Mother, Hafeeza.

Contents

Foreword

Written by Sabiya Mir, Bachelor of technology (Electrical)
Baramulla, Jammu and Kashmir, India
—193101

I was an average student in school with limited ideas in mind. Gradually, with time my intellectual
horizon started to expand as my mind got exposed to this vast cosmic ocean - the universe.
The author of this booklet is definitely encountering the different aspects of human perception.
What I personally like about this booklet is that it offers a scientific perspective into the behavioural
landscape of life via the short but insightful lines. I'm sure this booklet will force the reader to
consider a different perspective on, otherwise, well established and well excepted walks of life. At
the end what matters is that you realise your worth and role, as conscious beings, in the causal flow
of this vast cosmic sea. Let your intellectual horizons expand beyond the confined walls of servival
and social hierarchies. I remember being with the Author once and gazing at the night sky and was amazed to look at the sky from his perspective. I would often look at the night sky but that night while I was outside,Coincidentally, I was also on a phone call with the Author and While I was there he explained to me how these stars that I was looking at are millions of light years away and that the stream of photons
just hitting my retina had left their host star millions of years ago. Some of those Stars that I was seeing
were long gone and gazing at night sky, I was actually looking back in time. This completely changed
my perception of the night sky.

Preface

The surface of the Earth is the shore of the cosmic ocean. On this shore, we've learned most of what we know. Recently, we've waded a little way out, maybe ankle-deep, and the water seems inviting. Some part of our being knows this is where we came from. We long to return, and we can, because the cosmos is also within us. We're made of star stuff. We are a way for the cosmos to know itself. I've always been fascinated by the cosmic unknowns - the mysteries of existence. The best way to quench my thirst to understand this vast sea of existence & my place in it, I found, is the science. So every day I've to study & understand more and more and in the process, when the day is over, I'm equipped with a fresh prespective. Often I write these new thoughts that arrise from this new scientific information that I've gathered and this booklet is the collection of those cosmic brain droppings or thoughts. Hopefully, they will allow you to see some aspects of existence through a scientific lense.

Acknowledgements

Scientifically speaking, this booklet or any phenomenon that takes place in the cosmos, no matter how small or how big, is the product of the long chain of causal flow dictated by the laws of causality. In other words, everything that is happening or everything that will happen is, well, already set in motion by the laws of causality, destined to unfold in the exact same way that it will. Also, accourding to Albert Einstein's block universe, this booklet always existed, in these co-ordinates of space and time. So I don't really know who to thank in this acknowledgement.

1

I often think about the finitude of human existence & the infinitude of this vast cosmic sea, and the fact that I exist as a Conscious being, capable of pondering my own existence, never ceases to take my breath away. It's so strange how we take our existence & everything in it so far granted. What's even more surprising is the fact that we invent stories & goals to ascribe meaning to our existence, all of which revolve around the classic fitness payoff hierarchies. We are going to die, and that makes our existence as conscious beings very special. The potential people who could have been here in my place but who will in fact never see the light of day outnumber the sand grains of Arabia. Certainly those unborn ghosts include greater poets than Keats, scientists greater than Newton. We know this because the set of possible people allowed by our DNA so massively exceeds the set of actual people. In the teeth of these stupefying odds it is you and I, in our ordinariness, that are here. We privileged few, who won the lottery of birth against all odds, how dare we take our existence far granted & waste it living like robots dictated and directed by subjective hierarchies.

2

I've still not gotten over the baffling complexity of human life. Even some of the basic, everyday words that we us are so... complex. What do we mean by "knowledge" or "understanding"? And how do billions of neurons achieve them? These are complete mysteries that take my sleep away. Admittedly, cognitive neuroscientists are still very vague about the exact meaning of words like "understand," "think," and indeed the word "meaning" itself. I'm fascinated by this paradoxical complexity of human life & the recursive nature of it's complex hierarchies... Science tells us we are merely beasts, but we don't feel like that. We feel like angels trapped inside the bodies of beasts, forever craving transcendence.

3

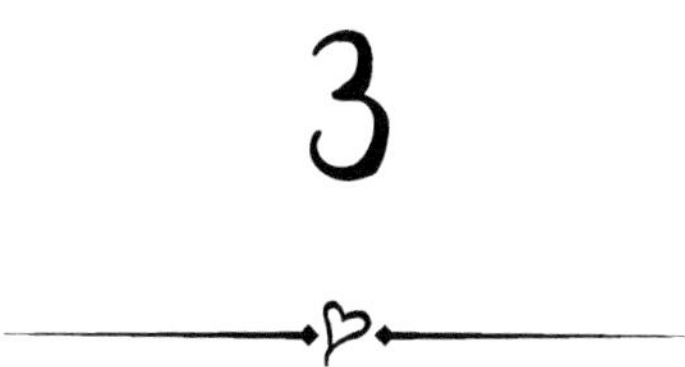

Will life in our Universe fulfill its potential or squander it? This depends to a great extent on what we humans alive today do during our lifetime. I'm optimistic that we can make the future of life truly awesome if we make the right choices. All the brake-throughs in science that got us out of the caves in first place, came from hand full of scientists, considering the total population of earth. There's one thing common among these handful geniuses, they chose to transcend the evolutionary limit of fitness payoffs & see beyond. Rest of us are so much occupied by the classic subjective fitness payoffs, like food, payments, sex, etc. that we become blind to other aspects of existence. Imagine if we had an economic system that covered all basic fitness payoffs of all seven billion people, all the mental capabilities of seven billion humans released from fitness payoff constraints to the freedom of thought, thinking & innovation. I can't even imagine the impossible wonders humanity could accomplish.

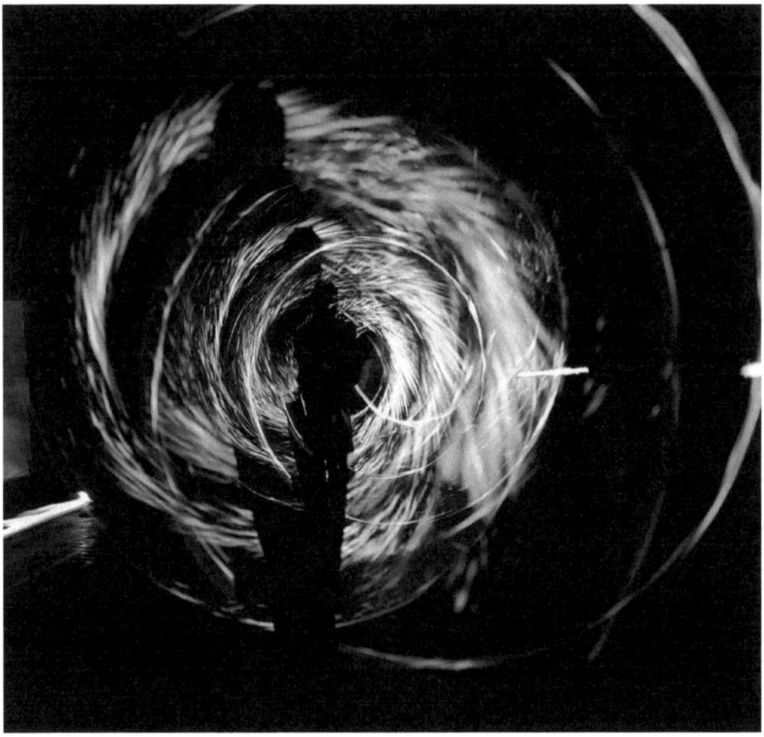

The interface theory of perception (ITP) claims that evolution shapes all sensory systems to be user interfaces that hide objective reality. A separate claim is that objective reality consists of conscious agents. We've so many theories trying to explain nature of reality but what if everything self actualizes? What if there is no objective reality? What if self actualizing packets of information give rise to new packets of information & what we call "Objective Reality" is this complex hierarchy of self actualizing loops of information. In fact, in physics, especially in cosmology, it's widely accepted notion that universe is made of information. In self actualizing loops there is no start or end, there is no first cause. It's a counterintuitive complex non-linear causal loop. And non-linear causality is counterintuitive for our feeble brains. In mathematical landscape it works perfectly in describing the nature of our reality. For instance, Bell's theorem kind of highlights the concept by challenging the notion that correlations should have straightforward causal explanations.

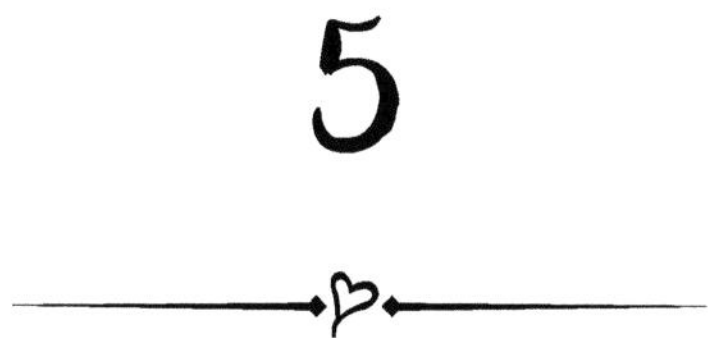

There is this recursive cycle in the realm of life that every system of life (by system I mean beings like humans) goes through, continuous repetitions with different conditions. For instance take an example of a Sheep, they are born they fallow the pattern laid by the flock, which carries survival points for the

Sheep. These patterns or ways are based on the accessorial experience. Now these experiences are drawn from ancestors living in different environments. Sheep fallow the pattern, mate & finally die. Natural selection has put a phenomenon called kin selection in animal kingdom, which in simple terms means that species care about their kin, like blood relations.

Life of a Sheep is like a closed system & every individual of the species can't do anything but fallow the circles of the system; Get born, fallow the accessorial patterns, mate & die & assuming sheep have some form of consciousness, may be experience some things while they're in the cycle. This is the golden rule of animal kingdom. All species fallowing an algorithm written by natural selection, incapable of questioning, understanding & exiting the system that they're part of. But after eons of causal flow & millennia of gene editing by natural selection, there's a Spark of choice in the kingdom of life.

Finally natural selection has managed to gather enough computation, in the brain of one species, capable of understanding, question & exiting this formal system governed by the algorithms of natural selection, Homo-sapians - the species that started as hunter gatherers & now has come a long way to master the mysteries of cosmos.

Enter Caption

I'm fascinated by the strange yet consistent patterns that dwell the realm of existence. Take any complex system, like; a human being, social structures often referred to as cultures, share markets, ecosystems, earth as whole or universe itself as one system. The word "System" is emergent, all systems emerge from the collective (causal & temporal) interactions of its constituents or variables. I've no reason to doubt that on a classic Newtonian scale every system is predictable given you have all the variables in hand. Every system that seems complex thereby unpredictable is actually the product of hidden variables. Let me elaborate, if you've system "Y" with ten variables let's call them "X", you know everything about system "Y", by everything I mean all it's variables & their possible interactions in all possible conditions. In mathematical terms Y = f(X), now if you know all possible interactions of all variables of a given system that means you know f(x) which in turn make the behavior of system "Y" not only predictable but exactly knowable. When scientists use this model to predict behavior of big systems like climate, they introduce another variables "E" in the equation, because they're Never able to predict the behavior accurately, so the equation becomes Y = f(X) + E, where "E" encompasses our inability to predict perfectly, Hence they declare the system as unpredictable. But I don't think classic Newtonian systems can be unpredictable, it contradicts the fundamental equations of Newtonian mechanics. The variable "E" is not our inability to predict accurately but "E" actually stands for what I call hidden variables of the system. For instance, if you want to take a bath, how many variables of water do you need to make the decision whether you want to take a bath or not? Well, you just need to know the temperature of the water. Now consider your bath tub as a system, the only variables of this system that you need is the temperature of the water, which also is the only variables accessible to you, but there are billions of water molecules in the tub, each molecule has velocity, momentum, the thousands of inter & intra molecular interactions, the bond energies etc. but all those variables are hidden & inaccessible to you. So if you have to predict the behavior of bath tub involving all those variables then you'll declare the bath tub as unpredictable because you don't have access to all those hidden variables. Every classical system that we've declared as unpredictable so far basically has some hidden variables in its f(x), hidden variables doesn't means we can't know them, it just means we've to understand the system on deeper level to know all it's variables, just like that tub of water.

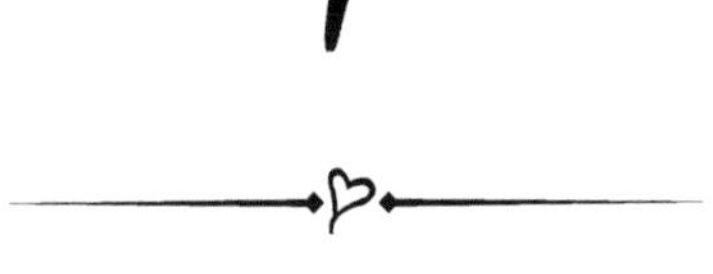

We're Machiavellian primates, our social interaction are very much governed by our past experiences. This is not true just for social interaction, everything we do must have a homomorphic analogue in our past. Let me explain, The normal way we conduct our lives is we reason by analogy. [With analogy] we are doing this because it's like something else that was done, or it is like what other people are doing. I think it's important to reason from first principles rather than by analogy. (With first principles) you boil things down to the most fundamental truths... and then reason up from there. Analogical thinking slows & in most cases shuts the door to new possibilities.

Enter Caption

Stop being patient and start asking yourself, how do I accomplish my 10-year plan in 6 months? You will probably fail but you will be a lot further ahead of the person who simply accepted it was going to take 10 years. And By plan i don't mean the classic fitness payoff hierarchy chase of animal kingdom, Try to see beyond the fitness payoff hierarchies . We should aspire to increase the scope and scale of human consciousness in order to better understand what questions to ask. Really, the only thing that makes sense is to strive for greater collective enlightenment.

9

Every percepta or emotion or feeling or any behavior that emerges from the kingdom of life is the expression of a complex chemical cocktail. For instance, when a male vole repeatedly mates with a female, a hormone called vasopressin is released in his brain. The vasopressin binds to receptors in a part of the brain called the nucleus accumbens, and the binding mediates a pleasurable feeling that becomes associated with that female. This locks in the monogamy, which is known as pair-bonding. If you block this hormone, the pair-bonding goes away. Amazingly, when researchers crank up the levels of vasopressin with genetic techniques, they can shift polygamous species to monogamous behavior.

10

If we don't perceive the objective reality, if our perceptions are controlled hallucinations created by the database of sensory inputs then why does the world appear stable to you when you're looking at it? Why doesn't it appear as jerky and nauseating as the poorly filmed video? Here's why; your internal model (perception) operates under the assumption that the world outside is stable. Your eyes are not like video cameras, they simply venture out to find more details to feed into the internal model. They're not like camera lenses that you're seeing through, they're gathering bits of data to feed the world inside your skull. Perceptions don't exist objectively outside the landscape of mind.

11

If you observe keenly the history of life on earth there's this weird pattern that dwells in every strata of life. Assuming the phenomenon of life has some sort of Intentionality behind it. If you start from Cyanobacteria all the way to Homo-sapians, three billion years ago earth was wrapped in a huge blanket of carbon dioxide, so the net effect was an almost inhabitable planet. The only organisms that could exist that time were single-celled organisms inside of stromatolites and other closed spaces. Lucky for us, one of those organisms that were alive at that time was Cyanobacteria. This organism has the special trick that we call "photosynthesis", the ability to take energy from the sun and transform carbon dioxide into oxygen and Over the course of billions of years, starting from two and a half billion years ago little by little these bacteria spread across the planet and converted all that carbon dioxide into the oxygen that we now breath . It was a very slow process. First, they had to saturate the seas then they had to saturate the oxygen that the earth would absorb and only then, finally, could oxygen begin to build up in the atmosphere. Just after about 900 million years ago oxygen starts to build up in the atmosphere. About 600 million years ago something really amazing happens, the ozone layer forms from the oxygen that has been released in the atmosphere. It sounds like a small deal, like we talked about the ozone a couple of decades ago but it actually turned out that before the ozone layer existed earth was not really able to sustain complex multi-cellular life. We had single-celled organisms, we had a couple of simple multi-cellular organisms but we didn't really have anything like you or me. Shortly after ozone layer came into place, the earth was able to sustain complex multi cellular life. There was a Cambrian explosion of life in the seas and the first plant got onto land. In fact, there was actually new life on land ahead of that. Nothing that you are familiar with today could exist without the contributions of those tiny organisms over those billions of years. Now, imagine for a moment that you were one of these little organisms two billion years ago. You might be born, you live a couple of weeks, you die and you kind of feel like, well, nothing really changed. I mean, I had no purpose in this life. Like the world I came to is exactly the same as the world that I left. But what you wouldn't have understood is that every breath that you took contributed to the possibility of countless lives after you, lives that you would never see or even imagine, lives that we are all a part of today.

12

The notion of "Self" as some sort coherent entity, the "I" with me is a merage. It's a paradoxical strange loop that reflects onto itself. Even if we don't go as far as Descartes's belief in an immaterial soul that somehow interacts with our body, it's tempting to visualize a dictatorial "self" inside our brain that is the locus of our self-awareness. Philosopher Daniel Dennett coined the term "Cartesian theater" to describe the supposed mental control room containing a tiny homunculus who gathers all of the input from our sensory organs, accesses our memories, and sends out instructions to the various parts of our bodies.

13

A universe without purpose should neither depress us nor suggest that our lives are purposeless. Through an awe inspiring cosmic history we find ourselves on this remote planet in a remote corner of the universe, endowed with intelligence and self-awareness. We should not despair, but should humbly rejoice in making the most of these gifts. As far as the subjective meanings & purposes of life that we manufacture or derive from the systems or patterns that we engage with in the unfolding of this causal flow, they're the functions [f(x)] of the type of systems and patterns that you engage with.

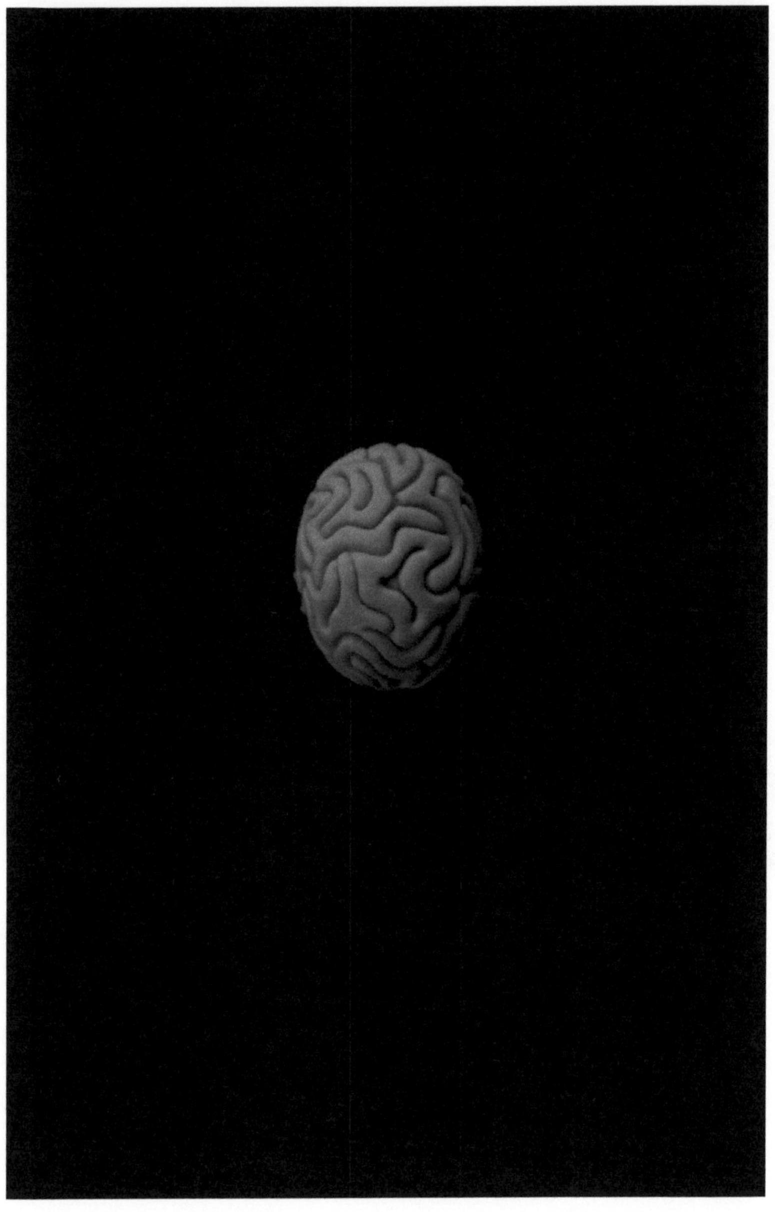

If I start with an axiom of consciousness being an emergent phenomenon then I can't Stop my mind from deriving these seemingly crazy ideas from this axiom. Emergence makes it all about the "Functional Organization in structural strata ". I personally like the concept of "Consciousness being an emergent phenomenon" it's simple (Occam's razor) & kinda opens the window for us to be able to understand consciousness. But at the same time it opens doors to some seemingly crazy ideas like that of "Panpsychism" or possibility of some complexly organized systems being conscious. For instance, if qualia emerges from this three pound mass of jelly, because of complex neural circuits and information processing then any system which can replicate that sort of complexity & information processing must be as conscious as a human being (The AI Singularity). These days we've even more complex systems like that of internet, millions of nodes connecting billion of processors, with continuous information flow & information processing at highly complex levels. Who's to say, internet is not conscious? Under the axioms of emergence I don't see how one can even argue this. You know what's even crazier, we're all on earth, seven billion people, doing our own things like those cells in the brain doing things dictated by laws of physics & chemistry, those cells Don't give a damn about you, they've their own, let's say, survival to maintain. The combined result of your brain cells doing their own things is your mind. So isn't it possible that all seven billion of us (complex conscious systems) doing our own things collectively result in some sort of "Collective experience", some sort of emergent phenomenon homomorphic to consciousness? Now, apply the same to entire cosmos...

15

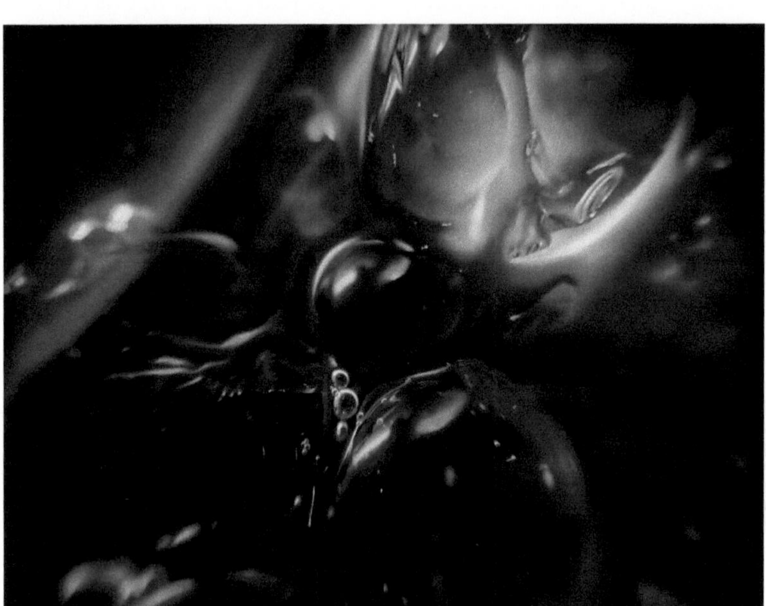

Consciousness: One among the few baffling mysteries of the cosmos. It is once the most familiar thing in the world yet most mysterious in nature. So what is it? Well, In my understanding, Consciousness is what transforms syntactical information into semantic information, it's what converts symbols into meaning & meaning isn't just another kind of symbol & it involves comprehension which is finding long range correlations between various meanings that are co-related.

16

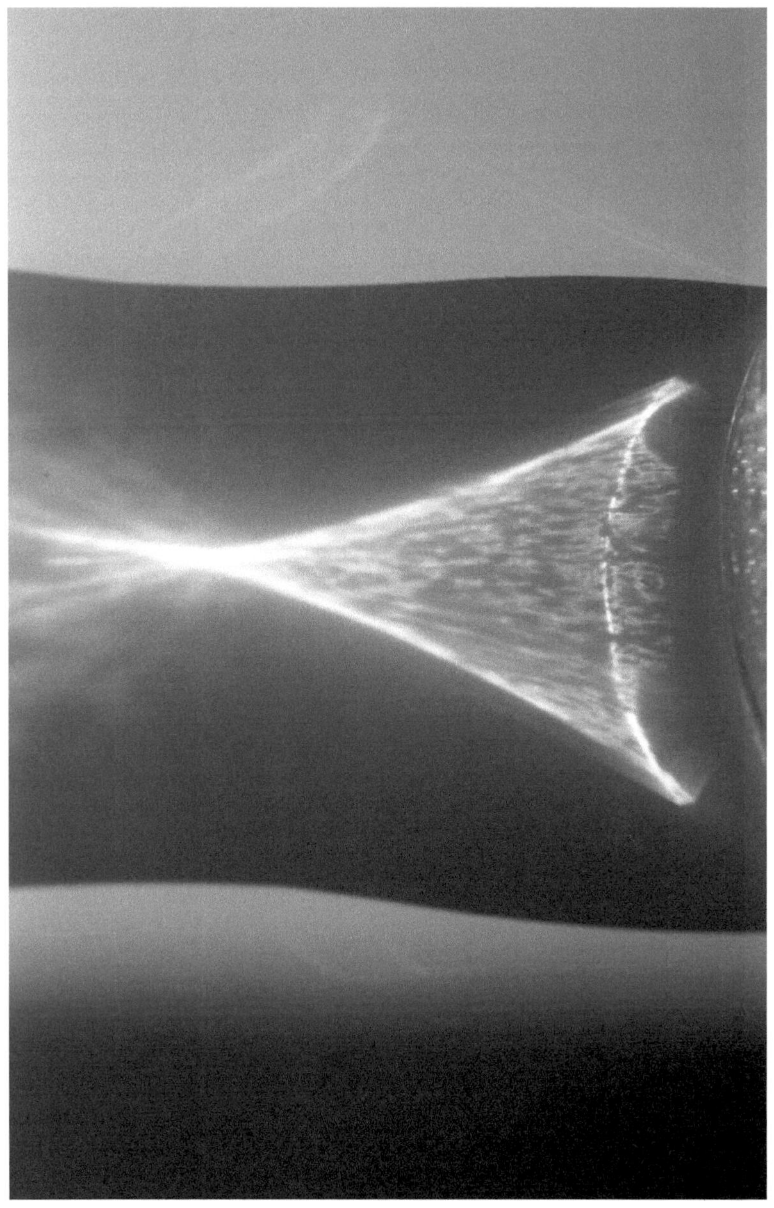

Contrary to popular belief our experiences, perceptions, emotions & feelings most of the time have nothing to do with objective reality, they're mere constructs - an illusory show put on by the exquisite neurochemistry of the brain. For instance, You can give me the most religions person in the world & the extreme atheist in the world. I can take them into the lab & literally exchange their beliefs & in terms of believing, turn them into each other for 10-20 minutes. Please keep in mind by above argument I'm just trying to point out how by activating specific circuits of the brain you can trigger different experiences & different perceptions in people. I am in no way implying anything about anyone's religion. Now, If an epileptic seizure is focused in a particular sweet spot in the temporal lobe, the effect is something like a cognitive seizure, marked by changes of personality, hyper-religiosity (an obsession with religion and feelings of religious certainty), hypergraphia (extensive writing on a subject, usually about religion), the false sense of an external presence, and, often, the hearing voices that are attributed to a god. SOME fraction of history's people like self claimed mystics and leaders MAY have had temporal lobe epilepsy... When the brain activity is kindled in the right spot, people hear voices. If a physician prescribes an anti-epileptic medication, the seizures go away and the voices disappear but also the part of their perception that was based on axioms grounded in that epileptic seizure also disappears. Our perception of "reality"(whatever that means) depends on what our biology is up to.

17

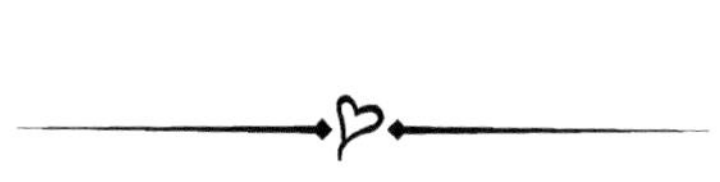

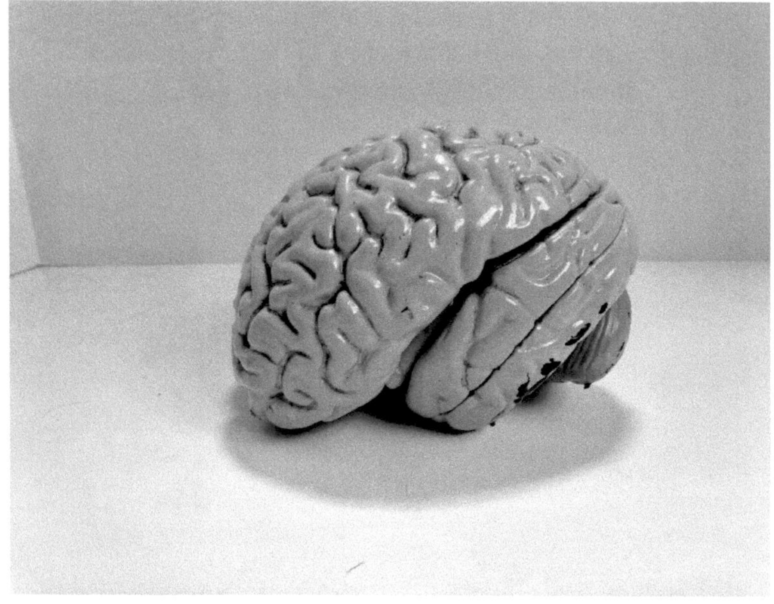

Human mind - The beautiful symphony sung by the neurochemistry of the brain. What a fascinatingly baffling system - Human brain. Brain manufacturers our perceptions, in a very active feedback relation with the incoming sensory data. All perceptions are acts of interpretation. They're acts of informed guesswork that the brain applies when it encounters sensory data. I think the way I can think of this is that there is no light in the skull, and there's no sounds. All that's going on in the brain are electrical impulses whizzing around in complex patterns. And out of all this - all this pattern-making in the brain, a world appears. Even the sense of "Self" the "I" with me emerges from this barrage of electrical impulses of brain, not just our percepta but the very interface of what we call "Reality" emerges from this electro-chemical, three pound, mass of jelly. When i think about brain & how it creates these perceptions even the illusion of "self" it literally takes my breath away... Nothing is as it seems! Not just what we call "Reality" but the very notion of "Self" is literally a mirage. Scientifically speaking, our perceptions are controlled hallucinations, We're all hallucinating all the time, when we agree about our hallucinations, we call it "Reality".

18

Keio
小田急百貨店
NIPPON
Tax Free
小田急
クリアランス

We humans create norms - arbitrary assumptions, social norms, cultural norms and somewhere down the line we actually forget these norms are arbitrary & they become rules that govern societies for centuries. They're mostly set forth by the generations before & we're born into them so they become the definition of normal & right for us. I find it fascinatingly paradoxical how an arbitrary axiom of previous generation becomes the governing fact for next generations to come.

19

One of the biggest mysteries that reside at the heart of neuroscience and lately, has made its way to Physics & Philosophy as well, is the question of how does matter generate the mind? if it does, because most experts believe consciousness can't emerge from physical matter. As baffling as this problem is, I think there is a homomorphic analogue that can provide some insights into this problem. Take an example of your mobile phone, it's made of Elements like Silicon, copper, lead, zinc, Iron, Aluminum etc.

forming circuits, transistors, chips and other parts of your device. Now when these parts & elements are assembled in a very specific configuration, the emergent result of all this is your device. Your device can now do things that none of those individuals parts can. It can process information, store & capture & transmit information. Of course, your phones or other device are much more simpler than a human brain, there is no comparison but the point is we've evidence, when matter is arranged is specific configurations it can do information processing, phenomenas that are nowhere to be found in the component parts of system can emerge from specific arrangement of the basic parts of the system. If we evaluate the above facts then it's not hard to understand how matter can generate the mind & consciousness. Of course, "How" is still unclear but we can admit consciousness isn't transcendent or non- local, it very much emerges from brain matter. You see, if you change anything in someone's brain, something about their mind changes. There are thousands, if not millions, of examples of such cases - all people suffering from any brain disorders. Everything you think, do & believe, the very notion of self, your entire interface of reality, emerges from your brain matter. And the crazy thing is your brain, although non-linear & enormously complex, is governed by specific laws thereof everything that emerges from it is not by choice or chance. There might be some syntactical freedom though.

20

The more I ponder the different aspects of existence, the more convinced I'm about the existence of one unified principal that governs it all. From cosmology to quantum theory to standard model of particle physics to biology to computer programming, there is a very subtle homeomorphism in all of these seemingly different and unrelated realms. As species, our interface of reality is driven by the vector of pattern recognition. We recognize patterns, name them, classify them but underneath our arbitrary classifications thereby identifications, I believe there is one unified principal that governs it all. I suspect there is one unified underlying mechanisms by which all that exists unfolds - from quantum reality to the large scale structure of the cosmos.

21

About every new generation that fuels the cycle of life; They may come as your sons, daughters, sisters, brothers or as any one you cross paths with in the circle of kin & relations. I want you to always remember that these are the sons and daughters of life's longing for itself. Just like when you came to life along with billion others of your generation & with your local, micro efforts you &

your generation re-shaped & replaced (technologically, ideologically, socially and in many other ways) the old ways of conducting life, even if the old ways made much sense to the generation before you, even if they resisted & protested against you for going out of "their" "normal" circle... Similarly, new generations with their micro efforts will, for sure, change the accepted & normal ways of conducting life but it'll be much more joyful if you accept & embrace it, even if sometimes things seem outside what you've known to be normal. Whatever is destined (causally) to happen will happen, you or I can't Stop it but it's gonna be a whole new experience if it's not resentful, toxic & is filled with support, acceptance & embracement. I want you to remember; New generations come through you but not from you. You may give them your love but not your thoughts. For they have their own thoughts. You may house their bodies but not their souls. For their souls dwell in the house of tomorrow. Which you cannot visit, not even in your dreams. You must not seek to make them like you, for life doesn't go backward, nor tarries with yesterday. You are the bows from which these new generations, as living arrows, are sent forth. The archer sees the mark upon the path of the infinite & he bends you with his might so that his arrows may go swift and far. You hold strong values in the chain of life. For it's only by standing on your shoulders are we able to see far & beyond. Each path to our new possibilities is carved by your hands. No words can express the gratitude we feel for your presence but as i mentioned earlier you've been through all this, you've done it already, let the new flowers of life bloom the way they know the best. Don't constrain them in your circle of "Normal" let them find new light that awaits them outside these circles.

22

Quantum theory; One of the crowning achievements of human intellect, yet no one seems to understand the meaning of QM. We do great in calculating stuff using quantum theory, however, when it comes to the meaning of QM, we have so many interpretation of QM that it have become the subject philosophy now. There are many interpretations of QM, most popular one is the Copenhagen interpretation & now a days "Many Worlds" interpretation has gained popularity, mostly because of pop culture, i presume. I like many of these interpretations & one such interpretation that I'm a fan of is Chris Fuchs's QBism interpretation of quantum theory, fan in a sense that I find it interesting, not necessarily true. In QBism Quantum states describe subjective degrees of belief about outcomes of measurements; each measurement creates new facts. Quantum mechanics, the theory we use to predict the behavior of elementary particles like electrons and photons that make up matter and light, doesn't actually pertain to particles, but rather to the beliefs about them of whoever is using the theory. And if several people are using it at the same time? Then QBism says that each of them is entitled not only to their own beliefs, but to their own facts. QBism interpretation of quantum mechanics basically takes an agent's actions and experiences as the central concerns of the theory.

23

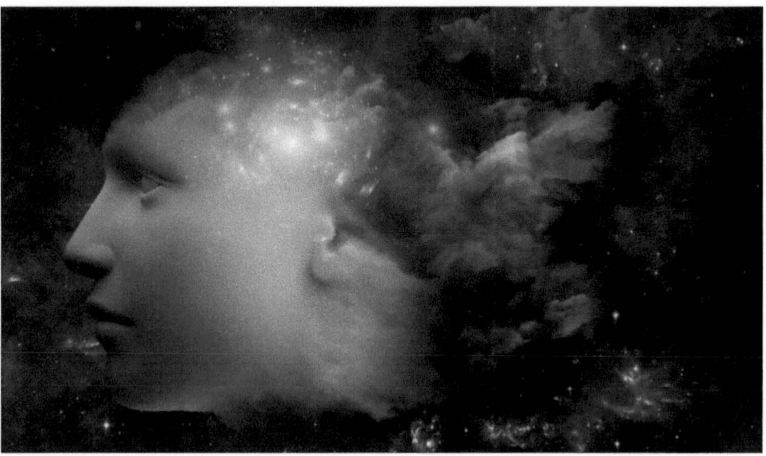

How does human brain give rise to the mind? In neuroscience & in science, in general, it's a million dollar question. It's touches some good old problems in neuroscience, like the hard problem of consciousness. There's so much literature written on the subject but just handful of perspectives make some sense, like Murre's computational theory in cognition or Emergence by Anil Seth & various others. But what actually is mind? Well, I define it in computational landscape, as a set of computations that extract any form of representations (such as percepta or thoughts). If you think about it all of our mind process such as perception, thinking etc, are basically centered on pattern recognition. We take inputs via our senses then the computation kicks in & not just any computation but computational nestled in complex hierarchies. Once inputs are in, process of inference begins, then we go through inverse reasoning, in case of visual cortex our brain does very complex inverse optics. The point is our mind is a set of computations designed to extract representations via pattern recognition. And If we can understand mind, in principle, we should able to write the code homomorphic to mind that is designed to extract complex representations through computations.

Wherever you are, whatever you're doing know this; Your existence is cosmic symphony sung by the eons of cosmic history. After Millions of years of gene editing by natural slection the arrow of life managed to arrive at the point of intellegence and consciousness. After eons of causal flow life was bestowed with the ability to trenscend the fitness payoff hierarchies through you and me, we Homo-sapiens reflect the spark of choice in the kingdom of life. But since we evolved from the beings that could not transcend the boundries of survival, somehow we've still chosen to be completely dictated by the fitness payoff chase of animal kingdom. Take a moment to understand your role in this vast sea of existence. With the intellectual capacity that you've been bestowed with, you can direct the flow of life in whatever direction you want. Among the millions of species of animal kingdom only you are capable of accomplishing intellectual wonders and transcend the fitness payoff hierarchies. Reflect on this and reclaim your ability to choose.

Printed by Libri Plureos GmbH in Hamburg,
Germany